# MARKETING SUCCESS FORMULA

Definitive Guide to Attract More Customers, Increase Sales and Profits with Less Effort

**RAJESH SRINIVASAN**

INDIA · SINGAPORE · MALAYSIA

## Notion Press

Old No. 38, New No. 6
McNichols Road, Chetpet
Chennai - 600 031

First Published by Notion Press 2018
Copyright © Rajesh Srinivasan 2018
All Rights Reserved.

ISBN 978-1-64429-532-8

This book has been published with all efforts taken to make the material error-free after the consent of the author. However, the author and the publisher do not assume and hereby disclaim any liability to any party for any loss, damage, or disruption caused by errors or omissions, whether such errors or omissions result from negligence, accident, or any other cause.

No part of this book may be used, reproduced in any manner whatsoever without written permission from the author, except in the case of brief quotations embodied in critical articles and reviews.

To my family and friends who stood next to me during the tough times in life.

# Testimonials

"The Four Step Marketing Success Formula" offers the marketers a tool in getting their products and services to the target prospects. The steps offered in the book comprise of simple, yet insightful, techniques and methodologies. I am sure, when implemented, marketers will definitely benefit from it."

**– Daniel Joseph,
Sales and Leadership Coach
(Author of the Book – Sales Pro)**

"Brilliant and easy to understand guide by Rajesh for any start up or an entrepreneur who is looking to expand his/her business. Absolutely simple and easily implementable ideas."

**– Sharath Kumar,
Regional General Manager – Sales
(Wipro – GE Healthcare)**

## Testimonials

"Rajesh's book 'Marketing Success Formula' has deep insights on how smart marketing techniques can have a direct impact on the sales and profits. A highly recommended read for start-up Founders, CEOs and Marketing Heads."

**– Kiruba Shankar**
**President – Professional Speakers'**
**Association of India (PSAI)**

# Contents

*Preface* ix

# SECTION – I

## The 4-Step Marketing Success Formula

| | | |
|---|---|---|
| Step 1 | Choose a Specific Target Market | 3 |
| Step 2 | Create a Unique Selling Proposition (A Compelling Marketing Message) to the Specific Target Market | 10 |
| Step 3 | Choose the Right Media Strategy and Show the Marketing Message to Your Ideal Target Market | 24 |
| Step 4 | Sell More to Your Existing Customers by Leveraging on Customer Lifetime Value | 37 |

# SECTION – II

## Additional Chapters

1. Apply 80/20 Principle for Better Productivity and Leverage — 53
2. 80/20 Sales Formula for Success — 63
3. Social Proof – A Powerful Way to Build Credibility to Your Marketing Message — 67
4. Celebrity Endorsements – 3 Things to Remember — 73
5. Be a Big Fish in a Small Pond — 75
6. Media Rules to Get More Returns from the Marketing Investment — 80
7. Grassroots Marketing – an Effective Way to Market a Local Business — 83
8. How to Get More References and Enable Word of Mouth Using This Simple Strategy? — 87
9. Low Cost yet Highly Effective Media Options for Small and Medium Businesses — 91
10. Three Online Marketing Tactics Which Businesses Can Use to Gain Credibility and Increase Their Web Traffic — 97

# Preface

## The Harsh Reality of Marketing

Dear reader,

Thank you for the time and attention.

In a highly distracted world, I know, attention is the most precious commodity, and I will do my best to justify your decision to buy this book.

Over the last 5 years, there is a question which has been persistently lingering inside me –

What is the basic purpose of marketing?

Why only a few companies generate more profits and revenues while others struggle?

Is there a way to eliminate waste in advertising?

Is there a proper way to approach marketing?

These questions have pushed me to study and research various best practices in marketing. One thought led to another and so on. I have had an opportunity to read some of the

## Preface

best books in advertising like *Scientific Advertising* by Claude Hopings, *Breakthrough Advertising* by Eugene Schwartz, and *Reality in Advertising* by Rooser Reeves.

The references from these books which were written more than 30 years back helped me gain critical insights about effective advertising and marketing. The real eye-opener was that while the tactics and techniques change over time – principles don't. If you base your decisions on principles rather than tactics, you can be the best in the market.

As a marketer, I can understand the challenges which you face as a business owner, entrepreneur or a budding executive. Though we come from different industries and markets of varied sizes, our problems are common and identical.

These are some of the hard truths:

1. Advertising is becoming ineffective due to media clutter and increasing costs. Though online marketing is cheaper compared to mass media, it is also cluttered with more advertisers.

2. Customers are bombarded with an enormous number of marketing messages that they don't remember most of them.

3. Competition is becoming huge across all categories. Now, consumers have more choice and less time to think and evaluate.

4. Conventional push marketing methods like cold calling, door-to-door selling is facing a slow death.

5. And finally, mass marketing is slowly becoming obsolete.

In this crucial backdrop, you need to have strategies that make your business fool-proof from competition and evolving customer needs.

Instead of looking for the next big thing or trend and become reactive to the competition, a creative entrepreneur needs to understand the underlying principle that affects his/her category and focus their efforts on critical elements. In marketing, a few fundamental principles govern the overall aspects of it.

Often, we marketers tend to correlate marketing with advertising. This idea leads to giving too much of importance to marketing mediums (media-obsession) like Print, TV, Social media, etc. Advertising is just a part of a bigger scheme of things in marketing, while marketing itself interlinks most of the crucial parts of other business functions such as product development, sales, distribution, customer service, and most importantly, finance.

This book has been structured to make you understand the strategic elements of marketing to ensure the most valuable outcome for the business.

It will address that one prominent concern every business owner has – 'Is the marketing efforts bringing results in terms of revenue and profits?' Everything boils down to this.

**Marketing Success Formula** – will help you to have a structured approach to grow your business. You need to focus

## Preface

on the crucial 4-steps which are presented in this book to create the right marketing plan which will help you to attract more customers, increase sales and profits.

I believe **Marketing Success Formula** will take you in the right direction whenever you face any challenges in marketing your business.

Come, let's begin the journey!

# SECTION-1
## The 4-Step Marketing Success Formula

A simple yet powerful
way to grow your business

# Step 1
# Choose a Specific Target Market

*There is only one winning strategy. It is to carefully define the target market and direct a superior offering to that market.*

**– Philip Kotler**

First who, then how

You will be surprised to know that most of the businesses or marketers have little or only a vague idea about their target market. Because of this reason, their marketing efforts (advertising campaigns and other activities) are not concentrated and directed towards a particular audience. This will not yield great results. As they are not very clear about their target market (whom they are selling to), they will not be able to write the appropriate marketing message which resonates with their audience. They will also end up choosing media randomly without having an idea whether their target market can be reached out there or not.

***The first step for successful marketing is to know 'who your target market is' and then decide 'how to reach them.'***

The market is diverse. It has all sets of people with various tastes, beliefs, needs and wants. Your product or service offering will appeal only to a subset of people. So, it is highly important to know who they are and understand them deeply.

***An ideal target market is a set of people who are going to get benefitted the most from you.***

**You can select your target market based on three segmentation strategies:**

1. Psychographic
2. Behavioural
3. Demographic

# 1) Psychographic

This method of segmentation is critical because most people make decisions based on their belief systems, motivations and attitudes. Understanding these elements will help to create products and services which will precisely match the needs and wants of your target market.

*Belief system drives human behaviour*

In marketing, a belief system drives purchase behaviour.

So what is a belief system?

To put it very simply, the **belief system** of a person or society is the set of beliefs that they have about what is right and wrong and what is true and false. (Refer: Collins dictionary).

Some examples:

Sam works as a general manager – marketing in a famous FMCG company; he believes saving and investing money in stocks will make him financially independent in the future.

Rick, on the other hand, works as the general manager – finance in the same company. He strongly believes that life is all about exploring and enjoying it to the core. He believes in travelling to adventurous locations.

They both have different belief systems (or values).

You can predict what Sam would do. He would most likely spend his time reading financial magazines and gain knowledge about the stock market. He would also talk to financial consultants to get advice on investing in the stock market.

Meanwhile, Rick would go online and make a bucket list of his must-visit exotic locations in the world. He would read travel blogs and magazines. He would eventually approach a travel company which specializes in adventurous travel and get an estimate for his trip from them.

**Now, you understand that the buying propensity of a consumer is related to his belief system about the category (product/service).**

See below how the market is divided based on people's belief system (A worldview):

- Quality conscious people Vs Price conscious people (People who buy Apple iPhone and others who buy Vivo, Micromax)

- Foodies (People who love food – most of the reviews in Zomato are written by them; they know which are the best restaurants in the city)
- Health conscious people (They spend time in gymnasiums, do yoga, meditation, and spend on food supplements)
- Entertainment freaks (The ones who watch all the movies and YouTube videos related to it)
- People who love travel and adventure
- People who value a better lifestyle (buy luxury cars, beautiful houses, wear costly clothes)
- People who believe organic food is good for health

Seth Godin, in his book, *Marketers are Storytellers*, calls belief system a 'Worldview' – the stories we tell ourselves. This determines people's day-to-day activities (what they see, watch, read and buy). A marketer's job is to identify stories which are prevailing in the market and fit his products/services into it.

From the 'Worldview' perspective, you can find various micro-markets and carve a niche. By realising that a set of people are becoming averse to allopathic medicines (a worldview), 'Patanjali' positioned its products as ayurvedic (with no chemicals) and subsequently became a market leader in this sub-category.

The marketplace is all about stories. You can observe what people are talking about on various online review websites, and observe comments on social media (like Facebook, LinkedIn, Instagram) and YouTube videos.

Segmenting a market based on psychographic variables can throw a whole bunch of opportunities for a marketer.

## 2) Behavioural

In any product category, few people will spend a disproportionate amount of time and money. You can divide a market broadly into three types of people based on their buying behaviour.

**Heavy users (Category lovers)** – People who love the category and spend most of their time and money (This can also be called your core market).

Take you as an example. What are the product categories you like the most? Where do you spend most of your time and money on?

As a marketer, it's your job to study the needs of the core market deeply and focus your marketing efforts towards them as most of the profits can be generated only by targeting this core market.

Why should you focus on the core market?

- They will be highly responsive to your advertising.
- They will be willing to spend more money on a high-price product/service.
- They will buy more frequently.
- Cross-selling and up-selling are relatively easier.

*Overall, with less marketing efforts, you can get more profits. (Leverage)*

You can identify heavy users in almost all markets. People who consume more ice-creams and chocolates, sports enthusiasts, movie-buffs and foodies are some examples.

**Passive users** – They neither love nor hate the product category. In any market, the passive users will be large in number. A marketer has to make consistent efforts to get attention from them and try to convert them to heavy users.

**Occasional users** – Special days such as birthdays, wedding anniversary, festivals (like Diwali, Christmas, New Year and Ramzan) are the times that these 'Occasional users' spend on a particular product category.

# 3) Demographic

Demographic variables are the conventional way of segmenting the market. (Age, gender, income, marital status, and profession)

Now, marketers combine demographic variables with psychographics and buying behaviour to get critical consumer insights.

The segment based on the 'generation,' which is nothing but the group of people born around the same time.

Gen Z, iGen, or Centennials: Born 1996 and later

Millennials or Gen Y: Born 1977 to 1995

Generation X: Born 1965 to 1976

Baby Boomers: Born 1946 to 1964

Traditionalists or Silent Generation: Born 1945 and before

Needs, preferences and beliefs of each generation vary drastically.

- Millennials are tech-savvy and will be the early patrons of most of the tech products (Generation X and Baby Boomers are generally hesitant to adopt tech products).

- Millennials spend more time on the internet than on other traditional mediums like newspapers.

- Traditionalists and Baby Boomers still spend time reading newspapers.

- Millennials, Gen Z spend more on life experiences (adventure and travel).

Instead of just segmenting the market based on basic variables such as demographic, marketers can club it with other variables like belief systems, buying behaviour, buying occasions, and generation which will give an overall understanding of the consumer. This will provide more profound insights into the target market.

# Step 2
# Create a Unique Selling Proposition (A Compelling Marketing Message) to the Specific Target Market

*The most common mistake companies make is to solve problems no one has.*

**– Paul Graham**

Keep in mind that your advertisement and creative (ad copy, layout, etc.) aren't more important than your audience or what you have to offer.

In the 1960s, direct marketing guru, Ed Mayer, coined **The 40/40/20 Rule**, which states that 40% of the marketing success comes from targeting the right audience, the other 40% from the right offer, and only the final 20% from the creative

Let me start this chapter with a small case study. In 1960, a small pizza company owned by Tom Morgan, the founder of Domino's Pizza, faced the challenge most business owners face – the challenge of differentiation. At that time, Domino's was just another pizza company in Michigan. Morgan wanted to increase the sales and grow its franchise.

## Create a Unique Selling Proposition

If you know the pizza market, you would agree with me that there is no major difference in quality. A simple blind test would prove this point. So, Morgan felt a differentiated value proposition would help drive more sales. He came up with a brilliant idea (in the form of a brand promise) that made Domino's what was a small pizza company in 1960's into a 1.4-billion revenue generating asset in 2009.

His unique selling proposition was:

"We GUARANTEE -
Fresh hot pizza, delivered in 30 minutes or less or it's FREE!"

FedEx faced the similar challenge and they took a cue from Dominos.

"Where it absolutely, positively has to be there overnight"

***When it absolutely, positively has to be there overnight –***
*This is the unique value proposition of Fedex.*

FedEx went from a small courier service to one of the largest companies in the world because of this unique value proposition.

Both Dominos and FedEx are big brands now but remember they were very small when they started. They didn't have much money to advertise; they had to fight for differentiation in the market. They knew they couldn't survive in the highly competitive pizza and logistics markets, otherwise.

They succeeded because they understood the importance of having a unique value proposition (UVP) or otherwise called the Unique Selling Proposition (USP)

So, what is USP?

The concept of USP was first developed by a television advertising pioneer, Rosser Reeves, in the 1940s.

In his book, *Reality in Advertising*, Reeves expresses his concern that USP is widely misunderstood. His major concern was that in advertising more importance had been given to 'creative' than to the benefits to the consumer. He studied all the advertisements and found out that most of them didn't carry the 'benefits' the consumers got by using the product/ service.

He came up with three basic rules for an advertisement that summed up his ideas about the USP.

## Create a Unique Selling Proposition

1. Each advertisement must make a proposition to the consumer—not just words, product puffery, or show-window advertising. Each advertisement must say to each reader: 'Buy this product, for *this specific benefit.*'

2. The proposition must be one competitor cannot or do not offer. It must be unique.

3. The proposition must be strong enough to move the masses, i.e., attract new customers as well as convert potential customers.

Based on this understanding, he created ads for his clients with USP, and grew their sales multi-fold.

Some of his USP ads that produced stunning results were:

Anacin (1950s) – The USP was *Kills Headaches Fast.*

For another chocolate company called M&M, he rolled out a USP ' *"Melt(s) in your mouth, not in your hand'.*

All these ads based on USP had greater advertising pull (response) and penetration in the minds of prospective customers.

**The starting point of any marketing strategy is to craft a killer value proposition to a specific target market.**

*The USP should also answer this key question: Why should someone buy from you instead of your competitors?*

## How to Create a Killer USP?

Two key things to consider when creating a compelling value proposition for your product/service:

1. It should be different from the competition (consumers should also perceive the differentiation offered by you).
2. It should be relevant to the needs of the consumers in your target market. What's the point in solving a problem for which there is no need in the market?

**Choose from the various categories of the USPs you can create**

1. Uniqueness based on price
2. Uniqueness based on what you sell
3. Uniqueness based on the guarantee
4. Uniqueness based on your target market
5. Uniqueness based on the time-frame you offer
6. Uniqueness based on the different experience and story

**Uniqueness based on Price**

You offer the lowest price in the market (Example: Walmart in retail, Google PPC ads, and Facebook in the advertising market, Uber/Ola in the cab rental services)

Offering a low-price as a USP is not a bad idea if you can reduce the cost of the distribution and operations otherwise it will eat up the profitability of your business.

**Uniqueness based on Guarantee**

What are the guarantees you can offer in your product/service category?

A powerful guarantee increases the confidence of the customers and will motivate them to buy your product. Especially, when you enter a new market, it will help to break the initial market resistance because consumers are fearful and have doubts about your company.

For example:

**For a hotel**

We will offer you clean rooms and friendly service every time. If you're not happy, we don't expect you to pay.

**Automobile service centre**

Still, have repairs after the service? Call us within a week; we will do it for free.

**Restaurant**

We give you the tastiest South India Thali in the city. If you're not happy, we will give you a full refund on your bill.

**Digital marketing agency**

Pay us only if we increase your lead-conversion ratio by 2%

You can base the guarantee on price, service, time and quality

Offering a bold guarantee will be intimidating because of two reasons: – You do not have the capability or process to deliver, or you think consumers may misuse it.

You need to identify the strength of your product/service before providing the guarantee. It gives you an opportunity to look into your overall operations and service standards. If you can find where your company excels in terms of product/service, you can offer that as a guarantee to the customers.

On the other hand, you don't have to worry too much about consumers misusing it. Because most of the times, consumers don't go to that extent (except a few). If someone misuses it intentionally, ask them to return the product. You can even blacklist them from your service.

When you provide a guarantee on high-value items such as machines, (in a B2B, i.e., Business-to-business environment), you have to insist to the customers that they follow the process, and inform them that failing to do so would result in forfeiture of any guarantee.

**Uniqueness based on Target market**

You sell to a very specific section of your target market.

Offering your services to a very niche market is in itself a USP.

The main advantage of this type of USP is that you can attract clients easily because your message and offer will be very specific to them.

For example:

Your digital agency specializes in creating highly convertible websites for the real estate industry.

If a marketing manager of a real estate company sees your ad and those of other general digital agencies, he will pick you because you offer a very specific service to him. He will perceive that you would give him a great website which will help get constant leads to his real estate business.

Other examples:

1. Cosmetic dental practice
2. Beauty salon for working women

**Uniqueness based on Timeframe**

You can also provide time-commitment as your USP. This assurance can be given only if you are sure about the internal systems, processes and have trained your staff accordingly.

**Some examples:** 24/7 customer support, on-time delivery, on-time cab pick-up, 15 minutes response time on email queries.

This USP can be applied in service businesses like hotels, restaurants, travel services, professional practices and B2B selling where customers are concerned about the timely delivery and support.

**FedEx:** When it absolutely, positively has to be there overnight.

**Domino's:** You get fresh, hot pizza delivered to your door in 30 minutes or less or it's free.

Both FedEx and Domino's are good examples of the USP based on timeframe.

### Uniqueness based on what you sell

Your product's special ingredient (like that in Coca-cola, KFC), heritage (more than 100 years old), originality (hair shampoo from the leaves of Amazon forest), could go a long way in reaching to potential patrons.

If you're selling fashion goods, answers to what type of fabric you use, what technique you use in producing it, are some of the things you can use as a USP.

### Uniqueness based on the different experience and story

Did you know how Starbucks won in the crowded coffee shop business? They have added 'experience' in coffee shops. They are not just selling coffees they are selling experiences.

Almost any product category can be transformed similar to how Starbucks did to the coffee shops.

You can add a different experience to a conventional product/service category. It will stand out in the marketplace and take your company to the next level.

Amazon did this in e-commerce (retail) through product recommendations based on the history of the purchase.

Other common USPs:

1. **Location** for real estate companies and hotels.

2. **Speed and convenience** – most technology brands like Uber and Ola thrive by this USP.

Be creative. Think about how you can use any one of the above USP categories in your business.

## The Significance of a Great USP

**A great USP will—**

1. **Help you to create better ads**

As I said earlier, most of the business owners and advertisers jump into the advertising and media part at the very early stage of the marketing. It's a very bad idea.

As Albert Einstein observed, "If I had an hour to solve a problem, I'd spend 55 minutes thinking about the problem and 5 minutes about solutions."

You should spend more time on thinking about a great way to solve your customer's problems (in the form of a USP) and then move on to choosing the right media.

2. **Help break the media clutter and get more mind share of the target market**

Today, consumers are flooded with advertising messages everywhere. No stone has been left unturned by the marketers to bombard customers with a constant flow of information or promotion of a product/service. When presented with too many messages, consumers get confused and avoid most of them.

Rolling out an ad with a unique and relevant benefit will solve the problem of breaking through the clutter inside the consumer's mind. When they understand your offer clearly, they will eventually remember your brand and prefer it over the competition.

## 3. Provide greater advertising pull and high return on investment

When your offer is highly different from the competition and offers a unique promise or benefit to the consumers, it gets more attention from the relevant audience and response rates of your advertising will go up dramatically. Because you're solving a pain point of the consumer which no one else (or very few) is/are solving in the market.

## 4. Help brands overcome the price war

One of the major challenges you face in any competitive market like real estate, travel, weight loss, etc., is that people choose a brand purely based on the price. This happens because brands are not able to differentiate the offering (commoditization). If you have a USP for your brand, you can get over this challenge of price resistance easily and avoid being battered in a price war.

## 5. Facilitate to focus company's resources around the USP

The best part of having a USP is that you can run the entire operations of your business based on your USP.

Recruit the correct staff. Train your staff and incentivize them keeping your USP commitment to customers as the metric. You can choose the right technology vendors who can support in delivering your promise to the customer. In a nutshell, you can simplify your entire back-end process of the business just by focussing on a few important things. This is very important because, most business owners focus on things that are not going to help increase their sales, profits and customer satisfaction.

Best practices of crafting a USP

- It should be specific. Don't confuse general brand slogans with USP
- Must directly address the pain points or satisfy the desire of the target market
- Has to be short and crisp which can be communicated as a headline in your ad copy
- Ought to be a touchstone for your organization. All stakeholders – employees, frontline staff, vendors, suppliers, distributors, product and engineering team, must be aware of this.

---

**Some powerful questions you can ask to craft a differentiated Unique Selling Proposition**

1. What unmet category need is my product delivering? (For example: I need full night protection from mosquitoes which the current 8-hour coil is not delivering.)

2. How is your product making people's lives easier/ better?

3. What convenience do the consumers get from the product?

4. Is there a negative perception of the overall product category your product/company refutes?

(Consumers have a negative perception about the overall real estate category due to the delay in handing over the homes by the developers. This is a good opportunity for a real estate company to find a unique position)

5. Are there specific usage habits that could be leveraged? Apart from making phone calls, people used their mobile phone to send text messages. Messaging was one of the features of the old mobile handsets and smartphones. The founders of WhatsApp unbundled this feature and created a separate application for the messaging service which is a big hit.

6. Is there a potential negative in your principal competitor's strength?

Rarely, people are aware of their own weakness, and it applies to firms also. If you feel that your competition's strength is, in fact, their weakness, you can leverage it by creating products accordingly.

# Unique Selling Proposition – Template

Step 3

# Choose the Right Media Strategy and Show the Marketing Message to Your Ideal Target Market

*"If you had no successful examples to follow, you need only observe how big business advertises and do the opposite."*

**– Earl Nightingale**

**Save more money and get highly relevant leads using Targeted Advertising**

You have to be very careful in media selection. Otherwise, you will end up wasting your marketing spends on it. The market is flooded with a lot of media salespeople who will try to sell media which might not be relevant to your business.

But, as a smart business owner, you have to use this simple rule to choose the media:

*While evaluating a media for targeted advertising, ask these questions –*

Will my target market read the content in the media?

or

## Choose the Right Media Strategy

Is the information published in the media relevant to your target market?

Marketing is a game of relevance. If you put your value proposition (or marketing message) in front of the thirsty crowd (people who badly need it), you will get a good response for your ads.

If you are a real estate developer or agent, you can start your advertising in the real estate and property sections of the newspapers, property portals and magazines.

Most of the business categories have separate classified sections in the newspapers. Some businesses like personal finance, beauty, healthcare, cars, bikes, spirituality, food, hotel and tourism have separate magazines (both online and offline) as well.

---

**Here's a list of ways to generate leads and traffic**

1. Google search/display
2. Facebook
3. Linkedin
4. YouTube ads
5. Search engine optimization
6. Ads in newspapers
7. Online classifieds
8. Niche magazines

---

9. Direct mail
10. Television advertising
11. Trade shows
12. Organized events/seminars
13. Billboards
14. Vehicle advertising
15. Leaflet insertions in local newspapers
16. Blogging/vlogging
17. Speaking engagements
18. SMS marketing
19. Networking
20. Regular newsletters
21. Write a book to your target market

## Master One or Two Media in the Beginning

One of the ways to dominate the market is to thoroughly master one or two media which can ideally fit for your business.

Given the media options available, it is almost impossible to be there on all platforms. You can win the marketing game only if you are willing to bet on a few mediums which can generate more leads and sales to your business.

Most entrepreneurs don't think on these lines. They randomly advertise in all the media (spray and pray approach) with the fear that missing out one might lead to failure. It is not true.

Most advanced and intelligent marketers master one medium to generate constant lead flow and improve their sales funnel (i.e., their leads to sales conversion ratio). They become extremely proficient in one or two media. It could be a combination of television and Facebook or Google search and some localized marketing.

Various combinations have to be tested to find out which media is working well for your business. It can be done in a few months by market testing. If you observe the data every time you run the marketing campaigns (response rates and sales conversion), you can find it out.

For ex: A restaurant which sells North Indian food might advertise on Facebook, the local newspapers, and leaflet insertions in a targeted location. Based on the response from each medium, the restaurant owner can put more money in the best performing medium.

## Marketing Success Formula

*Choose few media which get relevant leads for your business and then convert those leads effectively in the back end. Increase the spend (transaction size) of your existing customers. With the profits generated by it, go back to the market and spend money on getting more new customers.*

## What is the purpose of your advertising? Lead generation or branding

Marketers and business owners primarily advertise for two reasons. It is important to understand the distinction so that you can define your marketing objectives clearly and achieve results. It will also help you get more returns for every rupee spent on marketing.

1. Direct response advertising
2. Brand advertising

**Direct response advertising** (or direct marketing) is a kind of marketing that elicits a specific, measured response resulting from a consumer's direct response to a marketer. Direct response marketing is designed in such a way to facilitate a call to action from the prospect and outcome via direct or online interaction for immediate feedback and response.

Direct response marketing is used to generate leads and sales for a business.

**Brand advertising** is all about creating the right perception about your product/service in the minds of the prospective audience. The idea is to create a brand identity or imagery which will aid a future transaction. It primarily focuses on creativity and imagination.

Brand marketing requires a huge amount of money since it's aimed at the mass market, and media expenses to reach out are huge.

Brand marketing has to be done consistently because once it is stopped, the chances of people forgetting your brand are huge. That's the reason why famous mass-market brands like Coca-cola continuously advertise on mass media like TV and outdoor channels.

## Which type of advertising should you use?

Coca-cola, Pepsi, Nike, Dettol, Dove, Horlicks, Colgate, Britannia – these are some of the brands which heavily advertise in the mass media like TV and outdoor.

If you observe, these are all commodities which people consume for day-to-day purposes. These products are also low-involvement purchases, where the cost is low, and people don't do much of the research to select the product.

These products are for mass populations. So it should reach every one of them. Doing targeted advertising is difficult.

Brand marketers primarily look for brand recall and recognition.

The objective of advertisers is to ensure 'brand recall and recognition. In simple terms, if you think of toothpaste, do you think of 'Colgate'? This is brand recall. And if you are in the store to purchase the toothpaste, can you recognize 'Colgate' and realize it is toothpaste which you are looking for? This is brand recognition.

Brand marketers aim to stay in the top-of-the-mind of the market. That's why they never stop their ads because once you stop it, they know very well that people will forget it. It's the game of memory.

If you choose to carry out brand advertising, you should have deep pockets and be willing to spend considerably on advertising continuously, and you should also have extensive distribution networks to ensure the product you advertise is available across the market.

Strong advertising and distribution muscle is the name of the game in the mass product categories.

But, if you are an upcoming small and medium enterprise business, you cannot afford to do this type of brand marketing.

*Most of the Small and Medium businesses fail because they imitate the advertising style and pattern of those big brand marketers like Coca-cola and Nike. They might start out well but eventually cannot sustain in the marketplace. They run out of cash and eventually go out of the market.*

So, direct response advertising is the best alternative for Small and Medium businesses because if done properly, it puts money directly in the bank account

Benefits of direct response advertising

Lead generation

1. Direct response advertising is used to generate leads, increase traffic to the retail store, website. It literally means 'salesmanship multiplied through media.' It has an immediate effect on the sales and profits of the business. It helps business owners get rid of much-hated cold-calling (make unsolicited phone

calls in an attempt to sell something) and generate a constant lead flow for their businesses. The results are immediate. You put x amount of money in advertising and get 1x or 2x in return.

2. If you are a start-up or a small and medium enterprise, it's better to start with direct response advertising.

3. It is measurable. For every dollar spent on direct marketing, you can see how many calls, website or store visits, product trial, app downloads, you get at the back end.

4. The cost of producing a direct response ad is relatively cheaper compared to brand ads. Direct response ads are more formulaic in nature. In the direct marketing ads, an advertiser usually talks about the problems of his target audience and tells how his product/service will solve it. He will further give clear instructions as to how to get more information.

Big ad agencies usually produce brand ads. More importance is given to the creativity and aesthetics of the ad. Unlike direct response ads, they don't take a problem-solution approach. Rather, the focus is on brand imagery. So the cost to hire a creative agency and to produce ads are usually higher.

## What type of campaign strategy you must choose

If you choose to do direct response advertising with the sole objective of generating leads and sales, you could follow any one of these two common ways.

1. You can do a one-shot advertisement highly targeted to a particular audience with the objective to generate immediate sales. (or)

2. You can adopt a campaign approach with a follow-up sequence. It's generally called a lead generation campaign.

**Campaign strategy based on the customer behaviour and product involvement level (high or low) will fetch more results.**

Before we get into which type of direct response advertising strategy to adopt, let's look into an interesting aspect which determines the purchase decision of a buyer.

What category does your product fall into?

High involvement or low involvement?

A high involvement product/service is a category where the customers' exhibit extensive time/personal engagement and thought process before making a decision to buy. Because:

- The price is high
- It has complicated features and processes
- High-risk purchase
- The buying decision affects the lifestyle and values of the consumer
- Has more alternative products and services in the market

Some products/services which fall into this category are real estate, healthcare, cars, television, refrigerator, life insurance, consulting, etc.

**Advertising strategy for high involvement products:**

- Since people are going to take more time to evaluate the product and personally going to engage with the brand, let your advertising give some useful information about your product/service to the customer and ask them to contact you to get more information (Lead generation).

- Later, you can engage with the prospect and try to move them further in the sales funnel by showing how your product/service can solve their problem and how it's better than the competition.

Think of the two-step marketing process

- Lead generation to get relevant prospects.

- Have a rigorous follow-up strategy to convert them into a customer.

Remember; when selling a high involvement product, you should have a strong back end sales and customer relationship management (CRM) team with deep knowledge about the product and have good orientation towards customer psychology. Because, prospects tend to ask too many doubts, and clarifications about the product and your sales team's effectiveness in handling their queries will make or break a sale.

Even if you have to pay more, it's better to hire a great sales talent. Otherwise, your marketing efforts to acquire customers will become futile.

**Low-involvement product category**

On the contrary to high-involvement products, low involvement products are bought impulsively because the perceived risk is low. People have the habit of purchasing certain products routinely (like soaps, toothpaste, cool drinks, biscuits, etc.) and they don't use much of their time to decide which brand to buy. They buy what they buy frequently.

If you sell something which falls into this product category, your campaign strategy could be:

- **One-shot** (direct selling approach) in mass media. In the one-shot approach, your goal should be to reach the ideal target and do constant advertising to stay on top of their mind.

The objective of this approach is to generate quick sales. Your advertising here will talk about the customer problems; give some offer to purchase your products or utilize your services immediately. You will also give clear reasons to act immediately to grab the offer.

This can work only if you choose a right target segment, well-crafted marketing piece with the right message and relevant offer.

This one-shot campaign approach is ideally suited only for businesses which sell low-involvement products.

You don't have to generate leads because people buy these items directly from the shops whenever they need it. Since they are not going to do much of evaluation, they make purchase decisions quickly.

When advertising low-value products, you need to ensure it is available in the shops of the region you advertise.

## Marketing Success Formula

*Having a right advertising strategy based on the product involvement level and customer purchase behavior will yield a better return on your marketing Investments.*

**Ask these questions whenever you struggle to attract more customers**

1. Do you have a USP that nobody else in the market offers?

2. Is your marketing message unique or it is the same as everybody else's (competition) in the market?

3. A simple test to get the answer to the above two questions is: Take a newspaper and compare all the advertisements in your product category. Study how many businesses have USPs and a marketing message.

4. Does your marketing message resonate well with your target market (provide solutions to their problems)?

5. Is your media selection right? Are you putting your marketing message in front of the right (intended) target market?

The answer to the above four questions will solve most of the challenges related to attracting relevant prospects, increasing sales and better returns on your advertising spend.

# Step 4

# Sell More to Your Existing Customers by Leveraging on Customer Lifetime Value

*'The purpose of a business is to create a customer and grow that customer.'*

— **Peter Drucker**

Here's about what most business owners don't do that you should be doing to increase the profits of your business!

Most entrepreneurs focus only on customer acquisition that acquires new patrons for their businesses.

For ex:- If you are running a dental clinic, most of your marketing efforts are concentrated towards acquiring new patients for your business.

But the entrepreneurs of the most profitable businesses focus on one more area.

It is called Customer Lifetime Value (CLV).

## Understanding the Customer Lifetime Value and its impact on long-term profits

Smart Marketers use a model called Customer lifetime value to understand how a relationship with a customer for a longer time frame will have an impact on the profitability of the business.

CLV or Customer Lifetime Value is an estimated money value of a customer based on the period (time-frame) he/she stays with a business.

Most business owners calculate the Return on Investment (ROI) based on a one-time customer acquisition cost and value of the transaction. This type of measurement and thinking will affect the long-term profitability of the company. A smart entrepreneur has to see the bigger picture and ask the right question. What is the profit value of a customer if I retain him for a longer period?

According to the 80/20 principle, you can safely assume that 80% of the profits will come from 20% of the customers. The ratio of 80 and 20 might not be accurate, but the point is the majority of your profit will come from a few vital customer segments. This understanding is key to improve the profitability quickly and effortlessly. So it is important to find out who those 'star' customers are and divert your focus towards them.

### Marketing Success Formula

*You have to maintain excellent relationship with your existing customers (if not with all, at least with 20–30% of them who patronize you and continuously buy your products), retain them for a longer time, and sell more of your products/services to them at the backend.*

According to a report by Frederick Reichheld of Bain & Company, in most businesses, the cost of customer acquisition versus customer retention could reach as high as 700%

Fred Reichheld, the customer loyalty expert also observes;

- Acquiring a new customer can cost 6 to 7 times more than retaining an existing customer.
- Businesses which increased its customer retention rates by as little as 5% saw increases in their profits ranging from 5% to a whopping 95%.

Selling to the existing customers is relatively easier and will cost less. If you want to turn your business more profitable in a relatively shorter time and with less effort, you should focus on customer retention.

Moreover, with the data points available with you about them (like contact information, what products they purchase frequently, how much money they spend), you can create offers very specifically to suite their requirements and increase their buying.

I will tell you my own personal story here.

My wife used to purchase our monthly grocery and other items from a famous retail store in Chennai. She had been a regular customer of that store for two years. Her monthly expenditure was approximately Rs. 7,000.

Very recently, we shifted our house to a different location in the city.

The most important exercise I do as a marketer is to put myself in the shoes of the consumer while also wearing the hat of a marketer.

This might be a difficult exercise, but it will give more insights. Stepping into the shoes of the customer also gives an empathetic understanding of their expectations and pain points to a marketer.

So in this case, my wife stopped purchasing her monthly grocery from the retail store for the past three months.

But, there was no call from the retail store to find out why she has stopped coming.

They have missed a regular customer and have not bothered to find out the reason.

They possibly have not studied their existing customer data frequently to understand their status.

Not only in this case, but I can also give more real-time examples where businesses don't have any clue about their existing customers.

In most businesses like retail stores, two-wheeler and four-wheeler service centres, banking services, health care, there will be a purchase pattern where customers will utilise the service in a regular time frame. For example:

1. Monthly purchases in a retail store
2. Two-wheeler service once in three months

3. Car service once a year
4. Restaurant – once or twice a month

If the 20% of the most valuable customers are not returning to your business, you should find out why. The gap between the business and its existing customers should always be minimal, especially in the service businesses.

*You should know when your existing customers will come back to your business again and follow-up with them to ensure they turn up.*

Otherwise, you are missing a golden opportunity that will be grabbed by your competitors.

Here's a word of caution:

Remember, the more customers deflect from your business, the more you will have to spend on acquiring new customers. It puts your business in a negative loop where you constantly lose your profits.

It is like a leak in a water bucket. You may pour a lot of water at the top. But nothing stays inside the bucket because there is a hole inside it.

### Advantages of retaining your existing customers:

1. They consider your business and spend more money with you every time they decide to buy something related to what you sell. This ultimately increases the sales and profits of your business.

2. Happy customers spread the word and refer their friends and relatives to your business.

3. During tough market situations, when you struggle to get more new customers, your existing customer base will help you survive the downturn.

4. The cost to sell (advertising expenses) your products/services to your existing customers is very less because they already know about you.

5. Since they have already done business with you, the trust factor will be high, and further sales will happen effortlessly in a shorter time.

6. You can create new offers tailor-made to them since you know their requirements and pain points very clearly.

Now that you understand the importance of retaining your customers, you have to take some critical actions to ensure the same.

1. Maintain a database of your existing customers. There is a lot of Customer Relationship Management (CRM) software available in the marketplace, and it will help in recording the customer contact details, purchase history, etc.

2. Study the data more frequently to understand what products/services your customers frequently buy, spend more money on and when they last utilized your service. This can help you in inventory management, pricing and tailoring promotions based on customers' needs and buying pattern.

3. You should also look into the data of your existing customers and understand when they are likely to come back to you next time to utilize your service. This will help in avoiding the service lapses. If you are an insurance company, intimating your customers about the yearly premium deadline will help both you and your customers. For you, it ensures added revenue, and for them, no lapse in the insurance. They will definitely appreciate this. It's a win-win situation for both the customer and the company.

4. Stay in touch with them and find out whether they need any further service from you. This has to be done deliberately by your customer service staff periodically. Apple retail stores have an approach called 'anticipatory service.' Their staff doesn't wait for customers to initiate requests; they anticipate customers' requirements and provide service in advance. This strategy will wow your customers, and they will be motivated to use your service when you anticipate their requirements and serve them. Because they perceive you to be more friendly and caring when you call them before they call you.

5. Intimate about the new arrivals to your existing customers first before rolling it out to the market. If you're running a fashion or retail store, this idea could be useful and make your customers feel privileged.

Making money from your existing customers is as crucial as retaining them. It should be part of your customer retention strategy.

**Here are a few ways to increase the profits at the backend**

There is a marketing analysis tool which can help you identify the most profitable customers and focus your marketing efforts towards them. It's called RFM – Recency, Frequency and Monetary.

Ideally, using RFM analysis, you will be able to segment your existing customer data into

Recency – How recently a customer has made a purchase

Frequency – How often a customer makes a purchase

Monetary – How much money a customer spends on every purchase

How to calculate RFM scores?

You first need to have the values of three attributes for each customer:

1. Most recent purchase date

2. Number of transactions within a certain period (often a year)

3. Total or average sales generated through that customer

How RFM analysis will help you

1. Find out your best customers and focus your time and effort towards them. As you know, the people

who have already purchased your product are more likely to purchase it again from you.

2. Upsell and cross-sell other products related to what you have sold earlier. (more on this later)

3. Understand that not all customers are important to you. Very few customers bring most of the sales and profits to your business. This is a huge mental shift for entrepreneurs. Most of the businesses treat every customer in the same way. But don't you think the people who spend more money and purchases more frequently from you deserve more attention than the ones who purchase occasionally?

4. Segment the customers so you can carry out focused marketing campaigns tailor-made to their requirements – not random offers to everybody on the list. These highly targeted marketing campaigns will generate more responses even if the number of people on the list is very low because you are sending a highly relevant offer to them.

   Amazon does it extremely well. On successful purchase of a product, they recommend other products related to what you bought earlier.

5. If you understand the demographic (age, profession and other personal details) and purchase behaviour of your most profitable customers, you can ask the front-end marketing team to acquire customers with similar profile and behaviour.

## Applying the 80/20 principle and RFM analysis to increase profits quickly

If you want to put less efforts and get maximum results, i.e., gain maximum leverage in your business., you should definitely apply the 80/20 principle in all areas. The principle will perfectly fit into your objective of 'making more profits' in your business.

Here's how

If you study the data from your existing customers, you would observe

- 80% of the sales come from 20% of the customers
- 80% of the profits also come from 20% of the customers
- 80% of the problems arise from 20% of the customers (problem child)
- 80% of the references come from just 20% of the happy customers.

If you use RFM analysis and apply 80/20 principle on it, you will be astonished to see the scope of increasing sales and profits with the relatively less efforts. This gives huge leverage to you since you spend little time and money to generate more revenues.

*** Three revenue maximisation strategies for your business which will help your business to hit the pay dirt ***

### 1. Upsell

When you upsell, you induce the customer to buy a higher version of the product which has add-on features.

A customer enters a mobile showroom to buy a cheaper smartphone (with basic features), and salesman in the shop convinces him to buy an Apple iPhone by presenting him the added features and benefits available in it.

The idea is to offer customers a higher-version of your product in a suggestive way with an intention to increase the transaction size.

Upselling has to be done by thoroughly understanding the pain points and needs of the customer otherwise people will think you are blindly trying to sell something in the higher price range and they decide to move away from the business.

### 2. Cross-sells

Have you been to McDonald's? They use a marketing tactic more effectively than any other business on the planet.

If you venture into any one of their outlets, you would have encountered this key marketing principle which they use to increase their profits, which is nothing but 'Cross-sell.'

Would you like to have fries with that?

Would you like to supersize your meal?

You hear these questions from their counter staff frequently.

Why do they do it? Because that extra offer makes a startling difference to the bottom line profits.

Their billing staff is trained to do it effectively. If you notice, it will not look like hard-selling; they suggest it naturally and use it appropriately. This approach is called 'cross-selling.'

Cross-selling is nothing but encouraging a customer who has purchased a product/service to spend further money on buying other related and complementary products.

- Selling shoe polish to the people who have bought shoes
- Selling stabilizer to the people who purchased refrigerator and television sets

Such cross-sells will dramatically improve the profit-per-sale level of your business multi-fold.

Keep these two things in mind when you do upsell and cross-sell –

1. Context is more important. It has to be done at the right time based on the customer's need. Otherwise, it will backfire. People may feel pushy and become unhappy. On the other hand, if the offer is relevant, they will appreciate and opt for it.

2. Add-ons and recommendations can be made at the point-of-sale, and if you want the customers to take quick action, you can even offer a discount. I am not a strong proponent of discounted selling. But I am suggesting it here because you do not have 'customer acquisition cost' to the upsell/cross-sell since you have already acquired them.

## 3. Continuity Program

As the name says, continuity products/services are offered to the customers on the ongoing basis. Some businesses like magazines, gymnasium fall in this category naturally.

You can apply the concept of membership to almost any service/product business which has a continuous usage of the product.

In a membership program, you ask the customers to sign-up for an ongoing service on a monthly basis (payments are calculated yearly and collected upfront or on monthly basis).

This gives your business guaranteed and predictable monthly revenue.

Just think – how can you integrate a continuity or membership program in your business.

The concept of continuity/membership program can be applied in most businesses like retail store/saloon/training &and coaching, gymnasium, restaurants or other categories where the product/service is used on a continual basis.

---

### Have products/services at a higher price point

Another way to increase the value of the transaction is to have products/services at various sizes and price ranges. Most businesses have products only at the low price points, forgetting that people will buy high-range products/services if there is a need and if they see value in it.

You will be leaving a huge pile of cash on the table if you do not have high-value product or service in your business.

Remember as a rule of thumb; there will be a small set of customers who will buy high price range products/service to solve their problems.

You can notice FMCG product companies having product quantities varying from smaller to larger sizes (Soaps, toothpaste, beverages, etc.). Restaurants offer combo packages (bundling of various menu items). Travel service companies offer group tour packages.

It can be applied in small businesses as well.

If you run a grocery store, you can offer bulk orders for weddings, birthdays and other ceremonies at the wholesale price. If you don't offer this, your customers will go to the other wholesale stores to buy in larger quantities. All you have to do is to inform all your existing customers about the availability of the high-end offering. They will come to you for sure if you already provide good quality product and wonderful service to them.

# SECTION - II
## ADDITIONAL CHAPTERS

In the rest of the book, I will cover some strategies like 80/20 principle, niche marketing and other short-term tactics which you can use along with these 4-step Marketing Success formula to get better results from your marketing efforts.

# Apply 80/20 Principle for Better Productivity and Leverage

*"Give me a place to stand, and a lever long enough, and I will move the world."*

— **Archimedes**

The 80/20 principle was introduced in 1906 by Italian economist Vilfredo Pareto. He observed that 20% of the pea pods in his garden were responsible for 80% of the peas. Pareto then expanded this principle to macroeconomics by showing that 20% of the population owned 80% of the wealth in Italy.

80/20 principle states that few causes, inputs and efforts lead to the majority of vital effects, outputs and results. In simple terms, there are few vital things (20%) which are more important than the trivial many (80%).

You can find below some broad concepts which follow the 80/20 principle naturally.

**Input-output**

20% of the inputs create 80% of the outputs

Or 80% of the inputs create only 20% of the outputs

### Cause-effect

20% of the cause leads to 80% of the effect

Or 80% of the cause leads only to 20% of the effect

### Efforts-results

80% of the results come from just 20% of the efforts

Or 80% of the efforts lead to just 20% of the results

**80/20 Thinking and Analysis will be helpful in sales and marketing (also in other key areas of the business) to improve the productivity (that is less efforts and more results).**

In business and life, there are few vital things which are much more important than many other trivial things. But, we tend to generalize things and forget to focus on the relatively few important ones that change the course of our business and life.

We can produce astonishingly great results with relatively lesser efforts, if only we know what those vital few things are (and do it more) and do less or avoid the many trivial things.

From the business perspective:

If you deeply study the data and situations, 80/20 is there in every aspect of the business. If you want to produce astonishing results, then it's better to think in terms of 80/20.

Here are some of the areas in marketing and sales where the 80/20 principle can be applied for better results:

### Core customer segment

In any market, 20% of the people spend 80% of their time and money in a particular product/service category. Identify these heavy users and focus your marketing efforts on them.

### Product sales and profitability

Your business will almost have various products which cater to the need of your target market. Take the last month, quarter or year, and find out which 20% of the products produced more sales.

Next, find out which small group of products generate more profits (irrespective of sales). Sometimes, the product's sale volume will be less, but it will generate good profits.

*Action point:* You can direct your sales team to sell more of the profitable products, and reduce the advertising spend on less profitable products.

### Product features

Consumers give importance to only a few product features. They just don't care about the rest. Find out what they need desperately and focus your innovation efforts towards it. This will help simplify your product (like Apple) and give only what people want.

You can give prominence only to these features in your advertising so that it grabs the attention of the people.

### Marketing message

*Headlines* – Only a few words (mostly benefits) in the headline of your advertising create huge interest with your audience.

Few benefits of your value proposition interest most of the audiences. Find out that by doing a small research from the people who have already bought from you and use those benefits more frequently in all advertisements.

**Marketing Mediums**

Few keywords generate more traffic. Bid more on that keyword and ensure the top position in Google search. If you're doing SEO, optimize on those few keywords.

Few keywords get more leads and sales conversions. Find out what those keywords are.

In Google display advertising, few placement websites generate more CTR (Click Through Rate) and produce high-quality leads and sales conversions. Find out what those placement sites are.

Few billboards bring more footfalls to your store.

In TV advertising, few programs, time slots and ad creatives bring more response than the others.

Study all the marketing channels; you will be surprised to know 80% of the leads and sales come from just 20% of it.

**Customer lifetime value**

20% of the customers bring 80% of the profits. Pay close attention to them and ensure they don't move to your competition.

Very few happy customers (influencers) bring more references, write positive reviews and spread the word about your business. Reward them generously.

20% of the customers bring 80% of the problems. Find out these problem children. Be ready to fire them as they suck the energy of your entire team.

20% of the service-related issues create 80% of the problems. Find out the cause of those issues and sort them out quickly. These vital few problems are the reasons why your customers hate you. Solve it quickly.

## Action Implication

80/20 thinking and analysis will give you some groundbreaking insights into the vital few inputs, and efforts which produce huge outputs and results.

If identifying crucial insights is important, taking some action steps is even more critical.

**Action steps based on 80/20**

1. Shift your resources to those areas which are producing high results with relatively lesser efforts.
2. Stop doing low-value activities that are not producing results.
3. Reward the positive feedback/behaviour so that it produces more of the same.
4. Focus more on the strength of your organization and grow it exponentially.

Here's a simple request from me, don't enter into any business situation without thinking about the 80/20 principle. It will dramatically improve your productivity and help you get quick results with relatively lesser efforts and resources.

Come on, be an 80/20 person.

---

### How Steve Jobs' 80/20 thinking saved Apple from bankruptcy?

I am an ardent fan of the 80/20 principle. I wrote about this principle in various blogs and used it to solve many marketing and sales challenges.

I would like to share a short story about Steve Jobs's turnaround strategy in Apple where one can observe the practical application of the 80/20 principle.

Here we go..

After Steve Jobs returned to Apple as an interim CEO in 1996/97, the company was struggling and was starting at bankruptcy with overburdened product portfolio and expenses. The product line was labyrinthine with dozens of models across four vague categories (Macintosh, information appliances, printers and peripherals, and alternative platforms) operating in a commoditized market (with no product differentiation). On February 5, 1996, Business Week put Apple's famous trademark on its cover to illustrate its lead story, "The Fall of an American Icon."

In short, Apple was a hot mess in 1996.

Did you know what Steve Jobs did after his comeback to Apple?

Many observers and analysts thought Steve Jobs would develop advanced products; but he did an unexpected thing which any CEO would dare to do.

The following are the observations of Richard Rumelt, a business strategist on Apple's turnaround in his book **Good Strategy/Bad Strategy.**

"Within a year, things changed radically at Apple. Although many observers had expected Jobs to rev up the development of advanced products, or engineer a deal with Sun, he did neither. What he did was both obvious and, at the same time, unexpected. He shrunk Apple to a scale and scope suitable to the reality of its being a niche producer in the highly competitive personal computer business. He cut Apple back to its core that it could survive.

## 80/20 Thinking by Steve Jobs

Steve Jobs talked Microsoft into investing $150 million in Apple, exploiting Bill Gates's concerns about what a failed Apple would mean to Microsoft's struggle with the Department of Justice. Jobs cut all of the desktop models — there were fifteen reduced to one. He cut all portable and handheld models back to one laptop. He completely cut out all the printers and other peripherals. He cut development engineers. He cut software development. He cut distributors and cut five of the company's six national retailers. He cut out virtually all manufacturing, moving it offshore to Taiwan. With a simpler product line manufactured in Asia, he cut inventory by more than 80 percent. A new web store sold Apple's products directly to consumers, cutting out distributors and dealers. What is remarkable about Jobs' turnaround strategy for Apple was how much it was 'Business 101' and yet how much of it was unanticipated. Of course, you have to cut back and simplify to your core to climb out of a financial nosedive."

**Here we can observe 80/20 thinking at work:**

- Steve Jobs knew that only a few products were making profits. So, he retained those products and stopped manufacturing others that made losses.

- Most of the products in the Apple's inventory at that time were making huge losses, so he cut all the distributors and reduced them from six to one.

By doing so, he saved Apple from the brink of bankruptcy and also brought the renewed focus and energy back in the company.

You can observe 80/20 thinking at work even now in Apple's Marketing Strategy.

**80/20 in the product portfolio**

Apple's product portfolio is very simple and with clear market segmentation. The company has just 4 product categories;

iPhone (Smart phone market)

Mac (Desktop market)

iPad (Table market)

Apple Watch (Smart watch market)

**80/20 for more Profits**

This focused and simpler product portfolio has helped Apple cut down its costs (manufacturing, distribution), focus on creating world-class products, create a loyal following and improve its profitability. According to Fortune magazine 2017, it is the most profitable company in the world ($45.6 billion).

**80/20 advertising**

Observe their advertisements for iPhone (Benefit-based simple message. No clutter). They know that few benefits communicated in the advertisements would interest most of the buyers, so they have avoided all the unwanted stuff and made it clear. Again 80/20 at work

## Marketing Success Formula

If applied, 80/20 thinking and analysis can bring breakthrough results in your business also.

# 80/20 Sales Formula for Success

*"Sales is, first and foremost, a disqualification process, not a convincing people process."*

**– Perry Marshall (80/20 sales and marketing)**

Earlier in my real estate sales career, I used to be an abysmal sales guy. My sales conversion ratios were not impressive. I had all the tactical plans for follow-up and client handling. But, it didn't produce results. To put it simply, I had to put in huge efforts to follow-up to get very small amount of sales every month. A tough situation it was.

All I knew was follow-up and more follow-up (no matter the interest level of the prospect). The result was not very impressive, and I was going down.

But, I didn't give up because I was always passionate about sales and marketing. So, I started analyzing my own sales process.

It's a kind of self-analysis and observation from best sales performers in real estate and other high involvement ticket sales (like cars, insurance).

*I always thought 'I have to meet more prospects, make more cold calls – if I want to close more sales.'*

Breakthrough in my sales career came, when I understood not everybody who enquire (prospect) is going to buy from me. But at the same time, I have also observed that I was able to convince very few people easily to buy an apartment and convert them into a sale. Still, after 12 years, I remain in contact with them.

I again studied why more people didn't buy, and less people bought. Am I not converting all the leads effectively into sales?

Then, I realised:

Marketing and sales is a game of relevance.

All I need to know is – Am I spending more time with the high qualified prospects and engage with them deeply to understand their problems?

I have started qualifying the prospects based on the below parameters.

1. A strong need to buy

2. Money to spend(very important in most high involvement products like real estate, cars, insurance)

3. A good product-fit (homes I sold has to fit well their budget and other key requirements)

4. Whether they are decision makers (Have authority to decide)

I have eliminated all the prospects who didn't qualify on the above four parameters. Instead, focus on the few ones who desperately need what I sell.

This approach has brought in a huge number of sales for me with very less efforts.

For a sales professional, time is the most crucial factor. I need to know which prospect do I have to spend my valuable time with, so I can convert him/her as a customer.

As Perry Marshall in his famous 80/20 Sales and Marketing book observes,

***"Sales is, first and foremost, a disqualification process, not a convincing people process."***

For most of the time, we have been taught to focus on persuasion and convincing tactics like – Have a direct eye-contact with the prospects, have a firm hand-shake with him/her, be punctual, etc. But I have realized from my own personal experience, while all these persuasion tactics will help to some extent, it is not the only criteria for successful selling.

None of the world's most effective persuasion methods will help us if the prospect is not qualified to buy. It will eventually end up like this – 'Great Presentation. No Sale'.

It's not about how many people we have handled; it's all about 'conversions.'

As Shiv Kera (a motivational speaker and business consultant) observed, "We are not paid for our efforts, we are paid for our results."

The most productive sales people I know do the following things:

- They are selective. They don't treat all the prospects as same. They have a qualification process to understand which prospect will fit-in to the product category they are selling.
- After qualifying, they spend 80% of their time with this vital few (20%) prospects. Clarify all their doubts and queries. Establish rapport (persuasion tactics) for a long-term relationship.

> **80/20 Sales Formula**
>
> Only 20% of the prospects will bring 80% of the sales. Find out who they are using a stringent lead qualification process and spend 80% of your time with them. You will see yourself producing good sales with relatively lesser efforts.

# Social Proof – A Powerful Way to Build Credibility to Your Marketing Message

**Social Proof**

Social proof, also known as an **informational social influence** is a psychological and social phenomenon where people assume the actions of others in an attempt to reflect correct behaviour in a given situation. (Wikipedia)

Social proof is considered prominent in ambiguous social situations where people are unable to determine the appropriate *mode of behavior* and are driven by the assumption that the surrounding people possess more knowledge about the current situation than they themselves.

According to Robert Cialdini, who studied the principle of social proof in-depth in his book, Influence: The Psychology of Persuasion, "We view a behaviour as more correct in a given situation to the degree that we see others performing it." So often in situations where we are uncertain about what to do, we would assume that the people around us *(experts, celebrities, friends, etc.)* have more knowledge about what's going on and what should be done.

We human beings tend to follow the crowd (herd mentality). People tend to go to a crowded restaurant and buy things which others buy. This is a very powerful social phenomenon a marketer or business owner needs to understand and use it in their business.

I recommend these three social proofs which you can use in your marketing to increase credibility:

1. Wisdom of friends

According to the Nielsen Global Trust in Advertising Report released in 2015, the most credible form of advertising comes straight from the people we know and trust. Eighty-three percent of online respondents in 60 countries said they trust the recommendations of their friends and family.

The key thing to understand about recommendations is that it is organic and you cannot fake it. It means that you have to earn the trust of your customers. That's why it is powerful.

This leads us to one more important observation which is – most of the crucial purchase decisions are made outside the brand's marketing environment. It literally means customers' trust levels with their friends and other users of the product are higher than the brand itself.

So, focussing on better product quality, service and other critical elements which can boost the trust elements of the customers is critical for marketers apart from investing in conventional advertising.

## Social Proof – A Powerful Way to Build Credibility

2. Proof of your existing customers

Testimonials and positive reviews of your existing customers will also help in building credibility.

You can use testimonials which are nothing but the 'transformational stories' of your existing customers who have utilized your services. You could notice most of the brands using testimonials of their existing customers. But the most important aspect of the testimonial is that it has to be created strategically and has to resonate with the target customers whom you are trying to attract.

Follow these three strategies to create testimonials so that it can resonate with the prospects deeply.

- A specific pain point or a problem your product/company has solved to a particular customer segment

- Your Unique Selling Proposition (USP) which has helped the customer in solving his/her pain point

- Strategically choose the customers for your testimonials similar to the target market you are trying to attract. If you are trying to attract more CEOs to your business, have more testimonials from the CEO's who have used your services.

If you follow the above framework for your testimonials, it becomes very powerful.

Imaging this situation;

Your marketing message in the advertisement talks about the USP and the problems your product would solve.

Your prospect sees this and contacts you. Then, if he/she reads these testimonials (which talk about the same specific problems which you have solved for other customers), it becomes more believable.

These kinds of strategic testimonials can definitely boost the sales conversion ratios.

But, a word of caution. As I mentioned earlier, to establish trust, you have to deliver the stuff otherwise it will affect your credibility.

---

**Reviews in online portals**

Nielsen survey on Global trust in advertising also reveals 66% people trust consumer opinions posted online in the third part review websites as the key to their purchase decisions.

So, whenever you find a happy customer inside your business, you can motivate and reward them for writing about it in third party review websites.

Travel portals like MakeMyTrip and TripAdvisor provide user reviews to help the prospects in their purchase decisions.

---

3. The wisdom of the crowd

When lots of people are using your products, others tend to follow suit.

More social media followings, shares, likes, video views, more crowd in the retail shops/stores/restaurants will eventually attract more people into your business.

## Social Proof – A Powerful Way to Build Credibility

It may be difficult at the earlier stage of your business to have the 'crowd effect,' but you have to make consistent efforts at the beginning to ensure this is done so that people would perceive you as a business which is accepted by the others in the marketplace.

Marketers can add social proof in various other ways also –

1. Use micro-influencers (instead of a big celebrity since it will cost you more) in your specific field.

2. Talk about your customer base – if your customer base reaches certain numbers (say for example 2,500) share it on your social media page and website. Inform this to all existing customers so that they are convinced about their own decision to buy from you.

3. Motivate and reward your existing customers for writing positive reviews about your product in the third-party websites. The more positive reviews you have when compared to your competition, the better it is.

4. Have a live update on your website about user sign-ups, website visits, details of the visitors, number of downloads – this will dramatically improve your lead conversion especially on the landing page. There are various web applications available to do this.

5. Get your business certified by the industry bodies and rating companies. Using Trust seals on your check-out page can dramatically boost the conversions.

6. Take photos of celebrities who have visited your business and post it on your social media page and website. Showcase it in all the marketing touch points (Stores, office and other customer visiting places)

7. Media mentions – if your company has ever been mentioned in the media, create an 'As Seen On …' section in your website and use those media logos in it.

8. Talk about your associations with other credible brands. It will have a rub-off effect on your business.

9. Talk about the number of product sales that happened in a certain period (if the numbers are huge).

There is always a lingering question inside the prospects' mind about the believability of the marketing message. Adding social proofs to your marketing message will help boost responses to your campaigns.

# Celebrity Endorsements – 3 Things to Remember

While celebrity endorsement acts as social proof (we believe when some expert/celebrity talks about something it will be good) and increases the believability of the marketing message, you need to keep these three points in mind:

1. **Source credibility**: Credibility and values of the celebrity with respect to your business category (Viswanathan Anand is a good fit for NIIT (education business) –because he is perceived as a knowledgeable person, and when NIIT uses him, people tend to subconsciously accept the message because they want to become an expert in something after undergoing the course)

2. **Rub-off effect:** If used for a longer period, both celebrity and brands will have a rub off. During adverse situations, it could affect both the parties. In some cases, it has affected the celebrity (in the case of Maggi), and sometimes brands have also been affected by the negative image of the celebrities. (in the case of TAG Heuer)

3. **Frequency of the endorsements:** When a celebrity endorses many brands in different categories, the 'freshness' of the campaign will be lost, and people tend to confuse him/her with various categories.

Ironically, the world's top three brands (Google, Apple and Amazon – according to Millward Brown's 2018 report) don't rely too much on celebrity advertising. They make their brand and its value proposition as their central point of advertising.

If you can't afford to hire a celebrity who comes at a huge cost, don't worry. Think of hiring micro-influencers who are closely related to your product category.

- A famous chef would be a good fit for food-related products/services (Masala items, restaurants, catering services, catering courses).

- A famous and highly qualified architect or an environmentalist can endorse real estate players who sell apartments.

- Doctors are generally considered to market medicines and health food products.

You can even find influencers who have a huge following on social media platforms like Facebook, Instagram and LinkedIn and engage with them to spread the word about your business.

# Be a Big Fish in a Small Pond

**How to choose a niche market where you can be a king.**

If you notice, most of the mass markets are already matured and highly competitive.

Take travel services – Apart from the big players like Thomas Cook, Cox & Kings, SOTC, Expedia, MakeMyTrip, and Yatra there are a lot of local travel companies who market their packages to local customers.

The big companies have good money muscle to target the mass market using various television, print and online campaigns. You can notice they advertise heavily during the summer season (due to school holidays).

Tell me in this competitive scenario, how can a small and upcoming travel company do business?

There is a way out.

Focus on the niche market where those big travel companies don't specialize.

Some examples:

Become a spiritual tour specialist. You can create travel packages specifically for spiritual enthusiasts with some special services which they can't find in a general travel services company.

There is a famous saying in niche marketing which goes like this **'Instead of being a small fish in a big pond and be unnoticed, be a big fish in a small pond and get noticed.'**

What are some of the advantages in choosing a niche market?

I will use the same example.

If you choose spiritual tourism as your niche, you can be really certain about your target market and their needs and aspirations – which pilgrimage locations they love, the ideal time to visit these locations, etc.

You will be very clear on the demographic part like their age (mostly elders and people above age 30). Since you are very specific about your target market, you can also write a marketing message which can resonate with them.

**You can create a unique offer**

*'Book a spiritual tour to Rishikesh this year. Inclusive of free meditation, yoga classes in the Himalayas, and special veg food. Call \*\*\*\* – \*\*\*\* for enquiries'.*

See the above offer – how it is customized for a spiritual traveller. He cannot find this in a general travel company which focuses on exotic locations.

People are more attracted to the offering which is created just for them. They will get connected with you quickly.

## Media advantage

One more advantage in choosing a niche market is that you don't have to advertise your offering in the mass media to reach your target market (which in this case is spiritual enthusiasts).

You can choose media platforms where spiritual people hang out (think of magazines, special columns in news papers, TV channels that focus on spiritualism)

**If your marketing message is generic and not written to a specific target market, it loses its pulling power.**

General and vague marketing message will not attract the right people into your business. When you are a company that is already in the market and selling certain stuff, identifying a specific target market will not be a difficult job.

All you have to do is look at your own customers' data. If you notice a larger chunk of customers fall under some specific targeting variables, there is an opportunity to narrow your market further down.

Ex: You run a dental clinic, and while studying your existing customers' data, you have observed that there a specific group of college students aged between 17 and 22 years. You have further narrowed down and found out the reason they came to your clinic which was to 'clean their teeth and look beautiful.'

Here's a marketing opportunity for you:

You could create a unique offering which targets these college going students and create some compelling message like this. *'Beautiful smile without clean teeth will keep your friends away,'* 'Special teeth cleaning package for college and young working professionals.'

Since you have a *specific target market*, you can advertise the offer in targeted media where the college students hang out. It could be Facebook targeting or an infomercial (I will talk about what it is in the next chapter) on the television program which young students watch.

What you have done here is that you've created a niche market and an offering which solves the pain point of that particular market (You have applied a marketing success formula)

Think of which specific target group the main market has ignored in your product/service category which you can capitalize on.

## A simple research to find out the business potential of a niche market

Google Keyword tool would be highly effective in estimating the rough demand for your product.

You can go to 'adwords.google.com' and click 'keyword planner' option.

Then, click 'start using the keyword planner' and type your 'niche category' there.

For example:-

Paleo diet is one of the emerging niches. If you are a 'dietician,' this interesting and growing niche is a wonderful opportunity.

Google's Keyword planner shows:

10,000 to 1,00,000 search volumes per month for 'paleo diet' keyword. It shows how many people are looking for information related to that particular topic. (Data as on August 2018)

You can also find the search volumes of other related keywords like:

| | | |
|---|---|---|
| Paleo recipes | – | 100 to 1000 per month |
| Paleo diet plan | – | 1000 to 10,000 per month |
| What is Paleo diet | – | 1000 to 10,000 per month |
| Paleo diet weight loss | – | 1000 to 10,000 per month |

These search volumes indicate the market potential of 'Paleo diet' in the overall health and beauty market.

### You could also check the market potential based on

- Books sold in Amazon related to the niche.
- YouTube videos (check the number of views, shares and likes). You could also see the comments section to understand what people look for.
- Discussion threads on Quora and in other online communities.

# Media Rules to Get More Returns from the Marketing Investment

1. Success in advertising comes from three main parameters

   - Choosing a specific Target market (specificity is the key. Most marketers have a very broad target market)

   - Appropriate Value proposition & Marketing message to that Specific Target Market

   - Choosing the right media vehicle to deliver the message

Market – Message – Medium (all three has to fit together)

Before jumping into media selection, it is highly critical to know who your target market is (in terms of demography, psychography — their likes, dislikes, values, beliefs – and geographic area) and craft a message which makes them act immediately. You should also have an offer in the advertisement which is highly differentiated from the competition.

2. Show the marketing message to your target audience consistently.

Remember, in advertising, reach and frequency are the two critical factors of success. You have to reach the right target

## Media Rules to Get More Returns from the Marketing Investment

market, and you have to show your ads (message) consistently (not once or twice) to them to get more advertising exposure which in turn will result in more responses. This is more critical in highly competitive markets where more businesses advertise to increase their market share.

3. Any advertising you do outside your target market is a spill over and waste of your money.

If your business is hyper-local, i.e., a restaurant or a retail store which serves a specific locality, then advertising in a mass medium which reaches the whole city is a waste of money. You will be paying more to reach a lesser number of audiences in your target market.

4. Remember response is more important than the size and look of the advertisement.

If you have a limited budget, don't think about releasing bigger advertisements and releasing it in one shot. Spread your budgets for multiple releases on ads so that it gives you more response. It will also help in brand familiarity.

5. While Mass advertising (TV, Print & Radio) is still an effective way to reach the critical mass of your target audience, the cost to reach a consumer is increasing day by day. So choose ad slots in the TV/Radio programs which has some relevance to your target market. (For example: Marketer of a women's hair oil can release more ad slots in between TV serials which are watched primarily by women)

### Combine Paid, Earned and Owned media – A powerful marketing strategy

*Paid media efforts* – where you pay to get the space in other media. This type of media efforts should primarily be used for a lead generation which can bring revenue to the company.

*Earned media* – This is what the press and others talk about your company. As the name says, you earn it without paying anything (no advertising cost but you have very less control over the content). The impact will be very powerful when compared to the other conventional advertising.

Press releases about your company, interviews in TV, Radio, Newspapers and by other influencers' in Youtube channels, online reviews, likes & shares for your own content in social media platforms are some of the examples of earned media.

*Owned media assets* – Website, Physical or online store, office space, and other marketing touch points are considered as own media since you have full control over this.

*While **paid media efforts** drive people to your **own media assets** (people see your ads and visit your website), **earned media** will work as an incredible brand building tool. Credibility built through PR is always more effective, and you can use those media mentions (press releases and articles about your company) in your own media assets (like a website).*

# Grassroots Marketing – an Effective Way to Market a Local Business

SMEs and local businesses fail because they attempt to imitate the marketing and advertising strategies of the big-box retailers and national brands. The main reason why big brands advertise heavily on mass media like TV is that their advertising serves a broad market and it also complements their wide distribution and retail network.

If McDonald's buys advertising spots in a major entertainment channel, they spend huge money on the campaign. Since they have a lot of retail stores both at the national and regional level, their advertising efforts will pay off. But when the local businesses and SMEs with limited retail network copy the same idea, they are literally wasting their advertising spend.

So, if you run a local business – it could be a local real estate company, retail stores (like restaurants, provision store, dental clinic, saloon, stock broking company or any business which serves a specific geographic market – you have to think of doing grassroots marketing.

Grassroots marketing techniques are effectively used by politicians when they run for elections. Primarily, grassroots marketing is a tactic in which a business (it could be a local, national or regional business) can use to penetrate deeply into a specific geographic area.

If you observe most of the big businesses even though they have operations across their country of business, every store of theirs serves only a specific geographic market. They do it primarily by franchising their business to local small business owners. The parent company will have a marketing budget for advertising at the national, regional and city levels.

Two types of local businesses can get benefitted from grassroots marketing:

1. If you run a franchise of those big brands, it is imperative for you not to depend too much on the parent company's advertising efforts alone. You have to further go deep into the geographic area where your store operates to get more customers

2. If you run your own store with one, two or more business units in various locations in a city

Grassroots marketing requires more of an effort, and creative thinking than bigger advertising spends. If executed properly, it will give more return on marketing investments than any mass media advertising.

I have researched and identified some of the grassroots marketing tactics which you can use to increase the footfalls and enquiries for your local store. I also have a great amount of experience in creating a local business marketing plan and have training programs which can help business owners to learn this. I also consult big and small businesses on this.

> **Two low-cost and effective Grassroots marketing techniques**
>
> 1. One-to-one marketing
>
> Instead of relying on any media, you will meet and give your business card to at least one potential customer of your target market (in your location). You will have to give minimum 10 cards in a week and request them in person to visit your store.
>
> Jeff Slutsky, the local business marketing expert, calls this technique 'Business card handshake.'
>
> You have to give away a minimum of 100 business cards per month (3–4 cards per day). You would have distributed 1,200 cards in a year.
>
> This is what you will do. You will give a business card to a person by introducing your business and ask whether they have visited your store. If not, request them for a visit by offering them a complimentary service. If you are running a restaurant, you could offer a free starter; a dental clinic could offer a free initial check-up.
>
> Slutsky suggests giving complimentary offer handwritten on the back side of the visiting card by personally signing and giving it to the person.
>
> The response rate for this type of one-to-one marketing will be high because it is highly personal and people often respond to a personalized request like this.

They come and use the free offer and buy more from you.

2. Partner with other businesses who serve your same target market

If you are a dentist, you could partner with medical pharmacies.

If you are a marriage food contractor, you could partner with a marriage broker or astrologer.

If you are a real estate company, you could partner with a local real estate broker.

The thing you have to understand here is some other business is also serving the similar target market as yours. If you partner with them, you both can cross-sell your services. It's a win-win situation for both.

You could create a package voucher of all the related services and sell it along with your product.

# How to Get More References and Enable Word of Mouth Using This Simple Strategy?

When it comes to getting more references from the existing customers, many businesses focus on the loyalty program. The challenge with a loyalty program is – everybody in the market provides it to their customers (mostly credit-card companies and hotels).

While loyalty programs help in bringing more revenue from the existing customers by motivating them to add more points through regular purchases, they don't motivate them to refer their friends/relatives to the business.

I will share my own personal case study here.

My wife introduced 7 of her relatives to our family homoeopathy doctor, Sundar. This doctor doesn't have any loyalty program. He didn't even ask my wife to refer others. Then, how has he made it possible?

*He has delivered superior service to his patients and delivered results (cure from the ailments). His level of empathy is extremely high that if you visit him for the follow-up, he remembers your ailments (without referring to the case history). He has established a great amount of trust and credibility with all his patients because of this they voluntarily refer him to their friends and relatives.*

Big businesses often fail to understand some critical aspects of marketing which small business owners and self-employed professionals (like my Homeopathy doctor) tend to grasp quickly. This is primarily because these small business owners and start-up entrepreneurs lack resources (time, money and people), so they tend to think smartly to grow their business. They use organic ways (one that doesn't require money) instead of relying on expensive marketing tactics.

> **Steps to get more references effortlessly**
>
> 1. Provide great value and after-sales service (this will lead to better customer experience)
>
> 2. One area in which big businesses fail to leverage is 'Personalization.' Have a good one-to-one relationship with the existing customers. Train your Customer Relations staff to keep in touch with them frequently.
>
> 3. Ask for references – Train your customer service staff to ask for references from the happy customers (Yes, delighted customers tend to refer more people).
>
> 4. Apply the 80/20 principle and know who your best customers are – Find out the top 20% 'frequently referring customers' (Influencers) and pay more attention to them. Don't make a mistake of treating

> everybody the same way. Your best customers deserve more time and attention from you.
>
> 5. Remember, some people have good contacts, and they tend to spread the word about the products they use naturally. Try to identify these types of people in your database.

References don't work like lead generation marketing campaigns where you send some direct mail to your existing customers, and they start sending people to your business. It's more of an organic exercise. You need to have constant engagement with your existing customers – send physical greeting cards on their birthdays with free coupons, make an occasional call and find out whether they need any help from you or have a regular customer meet-up.

### *High level of engagement = More References/ positive word of mouth*

The right time to cross-sell another product and ask for a positive review/testimonial is when the customer is happy about your service.

Remember, unhappy customers, are reactive and will be quick to write negative reviews on online platforms, whereas the happy customers will remain passive and silent (This is a common human nature). As a marketer, you have to request your happy customers write a positive review/testimonials. You should make this as the top agenda because more the positive reviews/testimonials you have on Google Reviews/Facebook and other online platforms, more the trust that is established about your company.

*I always suggest businesses to allocate a small percentage of their marketing budget to WOW their existing customers.*

You can buy some gifts, tickets to movies or other local events or run contests regularly. This will help to engage with them informally.

# Low Cost yet Highly Effective Media Options for Small and Medium Businesses

**Classified ads – The most effective way to begin with newspaper advertising**

If you are advertising in the newspaper for the first time, I would advise you to choose the network of classified ads in the prominent newspapers.

Newspaper ads are costly and last only for one day. (Full page ads in the front page for a city would cost Rs. 25 to 30 lakh minimum, and the cost varies based on the circulation). At the same time, newspapers are read primarily by everyone in the family (especially the earning members and decision makers). So you cannot afford to leave that in your media plan.

As we said in the media rules, you have to be consistent in advertising. Since the cost of the classifieds is very cheap compared to the main advertising sections, you can potentially run several ads and maintain consistency in your advertising.

You can also use classified ads to test your marketing messages and offers. If the response rates and sales conversions are good, you can slightly increase your spend and choose some better positions in the same newspaper.

Most newspapers have a classifieds package (with good price offers) which will help you to release multiple ads.

You can release two types of ads in the classifieds section – Display ads and text ads. Display ads that can carry small creatives will capture more eyeballs.

Classifieds also have various sub-sections for small businesses like a car dealership, educational institutions, astrology, real estate, jobs, matrimony and business-to-business sections.

Since the advertising space in the classified ad is small, you have to choose your marketing message carefully. Otherwise, the response rates will be very poor.

You have to remember the main objective of releasing an ad is to get more leads for your business.

---

**Follow these simple steps to boost the response rates from the classified ads**

1. Your headline in the classified ads should capture the attention of the audience.

    Your headline and body copy (other sentences apart from the headline) should clearly state the benefit of your product/service.

> 2. Clearly mention the call to action and request for a response. Give the phone number of your business and mention the website address.
>
> 3. Give some offers like 'Free information session/Manual' or anything which is valuable to the prospect. This will also boost the response rates.

Remember the objective is to get calls from the prospects who are the relevant audience for your business. The challenge is – most of the times people are not ready to buy immediately. So when your ad appears in front of these people most of the times, they ignore it. The ideal way to get more calls is to take the educational route (that is to offer some content which helps the prospect in his decision making).

It means you offer some information for free to educate the prospects about your offering. If you are a life insurance agent, you can create a free report which says, "How to save Rs. 1 crore for your retirement with just Rs. 1000/- per month." You can advertise this report in the classified ads and ask people to call to get the free report or direct them to your website to download it. Before downloading it, you should capture their name, mobile and email address for follow up.

This will help to get more warm leads from your advertising. Whoever wants to get this free report is a prospect for your business. Some may choose to buy your services immediately, and for others, you should have an effective follow-up and engagement mechanism so that when they decide to buy, they choose you.

## Magazine Ads

You can find magazines almost on any topics – Entertainment, movies, cars, personal finance, travel, business news, spirituality, career, etc. Apart from this almost every industry has some kind of magazines for the insiders.

The cost of the ads in the magazines will be miniscule compared to other mass media channels like TV, outdoor and print advertising.

Since most magazines are centred on a topic and based on some interests, you can potentially choose one which fits your business. If you are a marketing consultant who serves only the car dealership, you can reach out to your audience by advertising in the trade magazine of the car dealers.

If you are running a stockbroking company, you could advertise in the personal finance magazine to reach the relevant target market.

Your advertising format for the magazine ad should also be different. People who read magazines prefer long-format articles. So, you can use this opportunity and release your advertisement in the article format with more benefits about your product and company.

They keep the magazine with them at least for a week or month and read them slowly at their convenience. They don't rush like they would do while reading a newspaper. So releasing a content-rich ad will motivate them to read and know more about your product benefits.

## Direct mail

Direct mail is one of the most powerful ways to reach out to your target market. Not only small businesses, but even big businesses can use this to reach out to their audience since it is more personalized.

Direct Mail is one of the old methods of advertising. When we didn't have internet and other technology tools like email, most of the communication was exchanged through this medium. You could deliver brochures, samplings and general information about your product/service to increase awareness or even information about store openings, events and coupon books.

### Advantages of the direct mail advertising

1. Reach the exact or the closest target audience.
2. Less cluttered when compared to other mediums
3. It's more personalized and reaches the house of your prospective customer and gets attention.
4. Less spill over when compared to other mass media like TV, newspaper and outdoor advertising. Direct mail can be more targeted.
5. The effectiveness of the direct mail campaign can be easily measured. You know exactly the number of audience the campaign is going to reach and based on the response rates you can easily measure the campaign effectiveness.

> 6. You can give more information about the product, images, testimonials, stories, FAQ in a direct mail than a quick TV commercial, radio or newspaper ad.
>
> 7. Since people receive the direct mail in their homes or offices, they can read it at their leisure and refer back at their convenience. People generally don't like to meet salespeople if they are not ready to buy, so direct mail is effective since they don't have to deal with salespeople and telemarketers.

In the United States, Burger King has been using a combination of surveys and in-store opt-ins and coupons mailed to customers over a specific geographic area to generate business. They are doing this continuously because it works.

Ikea – one of the world's biggest budget furniture retailers, uses direct mail to send out their catalogues to their targeted customers. They have turned their catalogue into almost magazine-quality pieces and send out frequently to their customers.

People generally ask me, will direct mail fit into my business? If your objective is to spread awareness about your product, drive people to your retail store or website, give out samples of your product, and generate warm leads — you can use direct mail, as long as you can identify a list of physical addresses of the particular set of a target market.

3. Publish useful content

When it comes to content marketing, most businesses make a mistake of writing 'about them' instead of providing content which customers are eagerly looking for.

We have to accept the brutal fact that people are not interested or too keen about the businesses. They only care about solving their day-to-day problems.

**Content strategy**

Your content strategy should revolve around this one thing – what are the customer's pain points? What useful content can we publish which can provide great value to the customers in terms of solving their pain points and requirements?

Three basic formats of online content

The content could be in the form of a

1. Blog
2. Video
3. Podcast

Pick whichever option can fit into your product category well. It's better to be adept in one form of the content and use it consistently instead of using all three formats inconsistently.

## Choose the Right Distribution Platforms

Once after the content is ready, you need to find out the right distribution platforms which fits your business category and relevant to your target audience.

**Your own website:** As the first step, you have to publish the content on your own website so that when someone searches the content online in the search engine, your website is picked up by Google. Even otherwise, the visitors to your website from other advertising efforts will also have a chance to read your content to solve their problems. The advantage here is that more the relevant content your website has, the more time customers stay on your website and engage with your brand. This reduces the bounce rate of your website which is nothing but people leaving your website quickly because they feel your website lacks relevant content.

These strategies would definitely help your company position as a great brand by facilitating constant engagement with the prospective customers online.

# Three Online Marketing Tactics Which Businesses Can Use to Gain Credibility and Increase Their Web Traffic

You can use these three techniques to establish the presence of your business online quickly;

1. Listing your business in other online platforms

In the pre-google era, businesses used to register in the physical version of the Yellow Pages in order to get found by the people who are looking for them. Now, there are more classified websites available on the internet which you can use to list your business, so that if someone searches your business category, you are easily found online.

You can register your business in the platforms such as Just Dial, Sulekha, Quikr, Olx and other specific online platforms which serve your business category (like 99 acres, Magicbricks for real estate). To begin with, you can choose a minimum paid package on these online platforms and can list your businesses for a year. These listings improve your online presence and help in spreading awareness about your business.

Core components of local listings;

NAPW – Name, Address, Phone number and Website URL of your business forms the basis of the local listings. You have to ensure that all these information are standard across all the online platforms failing which Google's algorithm questions the credibility of your business and does not show up in the search results.

2. Online reviews

The customers write online reviews about their experience with businesses. It can be about the price, quality, service levels and other things about the business. Today, most people base their buying decision primarily by checking the reviews of other similar users online.

As marketers, though we don't have any control over the conversation of people online, we can control the standard of services that are provided to the customers which will have a positive impact on the reviews.

But the one sad thing is, people will be too eager to write negative complaints than positive ones about the businesses. It's a normal human tendency. So, as a business owner, you should have a strategy to take positive testimonials of your customers and publish them online to review platforms such as Google, Facebook, etc.,

More reviews about your business will also help in search engine ranking.

www.ingramcontent.com/pod-product-compliance
Lightning Source LLC
Chambersburg PA
CBHW021544200526
45163CB00015B/1464